THRIVE

A Step-by-Step Guide to Creating Your Life by Design.

MB GUSTITUS

979-8-9928296-2-4
979-8-9928296-3-1

First edition 2025

Welcome to the THRIVE Journal:
Creating Your Life by Design

STOP.

Right now, just pause. Take a breath and ask yourself: *How did I get here?* And what exactly does 'here' even mean to you right now?

Look around—at your health, your relationships, your career, your finances, and your sense of spirit (whatever that represents for you). Is this where you want to be? And maybe the bigger question is, *When did I decide this?*

The truth is, most of us didn't decide. Somewhere along the way, life started deciding for us. Maybe it was the well-meaning advice of family or friends: *"You know what you should do?"* Or the cautious voices of doubt: *"Are you sure? That sounds too hard... you're too old, too young, too whatever."*

Feedback like that can act like reins on a horse, jerking us off course and making us take a different path, or forcing us to halt completely. And before we know it, years have passed—we're in a career we didn't choose, a body we don't recognize, or a life that feels like someone else's.

It's a lot like when you find yourself pulling into your driveway after a long day and thinking, *"Wait... I don't even remember the drive home."* Autopilot. Except we're not talking about your commute anymore; we're talking about your *life*.

If you haven't hit a major transition yet, just wait—it's coming. Life has a way of throwing curveballs I call the "7 Ds": **Diapers, Diamonds, Divorce, Disability, Death, Distance** or **Diversification** (think career change). These wake-up calls can leave us spinning, wondering how we got so far off course, like we fell asleep at the wheel.

Here's the good news: you don't have to stay on autopilot.

This Journal is Your Wake-Up Call

It's time to step into *your* own life with conscious intention. To choose *who* you want to *be, what* you want to *do,* and *what* you want to *achieve.* No more autopilot. No more letting life just *happen* to you.

I remember my own wake-up call like it was yesterday. I was 36, sitting in my first professional development class, when the instructor asked us to write down *50 things we wanted to do before we died.* Easy, right? I thought I'd knock it out in minutes. But by #3, my pen felt heavy, my writing slowed, and a quiet panic crept in. *How is it possible that at 36 years old, I have no idea what I truly want in life?*

That moment shook me. Up until then, I had been *surviving*—handling whatever life threw my way, reacting to challenges, pushing through. I knew how to be resilient, how to hustle, how to get through the tough stuff. But what I *didn't* know was how to *design* a life I actually loved. It took nearly 2 decades of trial and error, self-discovery, and a whole lot of rewiring, but I eventually found the tools to uncover my truth, break free from the limiting stories holding me back, and create a life that feels deeply aligned.

And now? I'm here to share those tools with you. Let's do this together.

An Invitation to Lean In

This book isn't about giving you a rigid, one-size-fits-all plan. It's here to help you get clear, get intentional, and take ownership of what's next in your life. It's a framework designed to help you define what success looks like for you, uncover what's been holding you back, and create a vision that feels deeply aligned with who you are and where you want to go.

But before we can start building that future, we need to get honest about where you are right now. That's what the first part of this book is for—to pause, reflect, and assess your current reality. Without clarity on your starting point, it's easy to keep spinning your wheels, reacting to life instead of designing it. This is your chance to stop, check in with yourself, and take a grounded look at what's working, what's not, and where you truly want to go.

From there, we'll start mapping out your next steps. You'll uncover the limiting beliefs that have kept you stuck, align your actions with your goals, and build momentum—step by step. And as life inevitably throws challenges your way, you'll learn how to adapt, adjust, and keep moving forward. You'll celebrate the small wins, too—because those are the moments that truly fuel transformation.

The fact that you're here, holding this book, means you're ready. You're ready to step into your life with purpose, to dream bigger, and to start building something meaningful.
So, let's begin. The life you want is closer than you think. All it takes is clarity, intention, and the courage to turn the page.

You've got this, and I'm cheering for you every step of the way.

Much love,

The 6 Pillars of THRIVE

This journal is built around six powerful pillars designed to guide you through your transformation. Each one serves a specific purpose in helping you create the life you want—intentionally, authentically, and with clarity. Let me walk you through how these elements will shape your journey:

● T : Take Inventory (Awareness and Reflection)

You can't change what you don't acknowledge. This is where we pause, reflect, and get real about where you are right now. By taking inventory of your life—across all key areas—you'll gain the clarity you need to decide what's working, what's not, and what needs to change.

● H : Harness Your Vision (Dreaming Big and Setting Goals)

Once you know where you are, it's time to dream about where you want to go. We'll dig deep into your vision, uncover what excites you, and set clear, specific goals that align with your values. This is about creating a future you're excited to live, one that reflects what truly matters to you.

● R : Reflect & Release (Clearing Limiting Beliefs)

Let's be honest—your biggest roadblocks often come from within. In this step, you'll uncover the limiting beliefs and old stories that are holding you back. We'll work on letting those go, clearing the path for growth and possibility.

● I : Intentional Action (Daily Habits and Small Steps)

Big dreams are built one small step at a time. Here's where you'll create a plan and take intentional action. With daily habits, routines, and consistency, you'll start moving the needle toward your goals—one day, one win at a time.

● V : Value Alignment (Living Authentically)

True transformation happens when your actions reflect your core values. This step will help you check in with yourself and ensure the life you're creating feels authentic, fulfilling, and aligned with what matters most to you.

● E : Evolve (Celebrate Wins, Adapt, and Grow)

Transformation is a journey, not a one-and-done event. You'll take time to celebrate your wins, learn from challenges, and adapt as you go. Growth isn't about perfection—it's about progress, and this step reminds you to keep evolving into the best version of yourself.

These Pillars aren't just words—they're the roadmap to your transformation. They'll give you the structure, support, and inspiration to move forward with clarity and confidence. As you work through each section, lean into the process, trust yourself, and remember: you're creating a life by design, one intentional step at a time. You've got this!

Take Inventory :
Awareness and Reflection

Before you can design the life you want, it's essential to know where you're starting from. This is the *Take Inventory* part of your journey—the foundation of the THRIVE process. Think of it as hitting pause and taking a snapshot of your life as it is today. This isn't about judgment or perfection; it's about honesty and awareness. By getting real with yourself, you can uncover the truth of where you are, where you want to go, and what might be standing in your way. Without this clarity, it's like trying to build a house without first laying a solid foundation. Awareness is the first and most important step toward meaningful change.

In this section, you'll assess seven key areas of your life: physical health, mental and emotional well-being, relationships, career, finances, personal growth, and sense of spirit or purpose. For each area, you'll reflect on where you are right now, where you want to be in one year, and why that goal matters to you. Your "why" is the fuel that will keep you moving forward, especially when things get tough. By the end of this assessment, you'll have a clear, honest view of your current reality and the roadmap to begin designing a life that aligns with your values and aspirations. This is your moment to pause, reflect, and take control of your journey.

Let's get started.

TAKE INVENTORY: AWARENESS AND REFLECTION
PHYSICAL / MENTAL WELLBEING

Take a moment to reflect deeply and honestly as you answer the following questions. These will help you gain clarity on where you are right now and create a clear vision for where you want to go.

On a scale of 1-10 (10 being completely satisfied), where would you rate your satisfaction with this area of life RIGHT NOW?

1 2 3 4 5 6 7 8 9 10

- *What does this area of my life currently look and feel like?*
- *What's working well?*
- *What's not working or feels out of alignment?*

Where Do I Want to Be in One Year?
- *What specific improvements or changes do I want to see in this area?*
- *How do I want to feel in this area of my life one year from now?*
- *What would success in this area look like to me?*

If I were to achieve this vision, what would I rate this area of my life then on the same 1-10 scale?

1 2 3 4 5 6 7 8 9 10

TAKE INVENTORY: AWARENESS AND REFLECTION
PHYSICAL / MENTAL WELLBEING

Why Does This Matter to Me?

- *Why is this goal or change important to me?*
- *How would achieving this improve my life overall?*
- *What's at stake if I stay where I am?*
- *Who else am I impacting if this change is made or not made?*

What's Holding Me Back?

- *Are there habits, beliefs, or fears that might be getting in my way?*
- *What limiting stories do I need to let go of to move forward?*

My Goals for this area for the next 12 months

- ◎
- ◎
- ◎
- ◎
- ◎

TAKE INVENTORY: AWARENESS AND REFLECTION
PERSONAL GROWTH

Take a moment to reflect deeply and honestly as you answer the following questions. These will help you gain clarity on where you are right now and create a clear vision for where you want to go.

On a scale of 1-10 (10 being completely satisfied), where would you rate your satisfaction with this area of life RIGHT NOW?

1 2 3 4 5 6 7 8 9 10

- *What does this area of my life currently look and feel like?*
- *What's working well?*
- *What's not working or feels out of alignment?*

_____

_____

_____

_____

_____

Where Do I Want to Be in One Year?
- *What specific improvements or changes do I want to see in this area?*
- *How do I want to feel in this area of my life one year from now?*
- *What would success in this area look like to me?*

_____

_____

_____

_____

_____

If I were to achieve this vision, what would I rate this area of my life then on the same 1-10 scale?

1 2 3 4 5 6 7 8 9 10

_____

_____

_____

TAKE INVENTORY: AWARENESS AND REFLECTION
PERSONAL GROWTH

Why Does This Matter to Me?

- *Why is this goal or change important to me?*
- *How would achieving this improve my life overall?*
- *What's at stake if I stay where I am?*
- *Who else am I impacting if this change is made or not made?*

What's Holding Me Back?

- *Are there habits, beliefs, or fears that might be getting in my way?*
- *What limiting stories do I need to let go of to move forward?*

My Goals for this area for the next 12 months

- ◎
- ◎
- ◎
- ◎
- ◎

TAKE INVENTORY: AWARENESS AND REFLECTION
KEY INTIMATE RELATIONSHIPS

Take a moment to reflect deeply and honestly as you answer the following questions. These will help you gain clarity on where you are right now and create a clear vision for where you want to go.

On a scale of 1-10 (10 being completely satisfied), where would you rate your satisfaction with this area of life RIGHT NOW?

1 2 3 4 5 6 7 8 9 10

- *What does this area of my life currently look and feel like?*
- *What's working well?*
- *What's not working or feels out of alignment?*

Where Do I Want to Be in One Year?
- *What specific improvements or changes do I want to see in this area?*
- *How do I want to feel in this area of my life one year from now?*
- *What would success in this area look like to me?*

If I were to achieve this vision, what would I rate this area of my life then on the same 1-10 scale?

1 2 3 4 5 6 7 8 9 10

TAKE INVENTORY: AWARENESS AND REFLECTION
KEY INTIMATE RELATIONSHIPS

Why Does This Matter to Me?

- *Why is this goal or change important to me?*
- *How would achieving this improve my life overall?*
- *What's at stake if I stay where I am?*
- *Who else am I impacting if this change is made or not made?*

What's Holding Me Back?

- *Are there habits, beliefs, or fears that might be getting in my way?*
- *What limiting stories do I need to let go of to move forward?*

My Goals for this area for the next 12 months

◎

◎

◎

◎

◎

TAKE INVENTORY: AWARENESS AND REFLECTION
FAMILY/FRIENDS

Take a moment to reflect deeply and honestly as you answer the following questions. These will help you gain clarity on where you are right now and create a clear vision for where you want to go.

On a scale of 1-10 (10 being completely satisfied), where would you rate your satisfaction with this area of life RIGHT NOW?

1 2 3 4 5 6 7 8 9 10

- *What does this area of my life currently look and feel like?*
- *What's working well?*
- *What's not working or feels out of alignment?*

Where Do I Want to Be in One Year?
- *What specific improvements or changes do I want to see in this area?*
- *How do I want to feel in this area of my life one year from now?*
- *What would success in this area look like to me?*

If I were to achieve this vision, what would I rate this area of my life then on the same 1-10 scale?

1 2 3 4 5 6 7 8 9 10

TAKE INVENTORY: AWARENESS AND REFLECTION
FAMILY/FRIENDS

Why Does This Matter to Me?

- *Why is this goal or change important to me?*
- *How would achieving this improve my life overall?*
- *What's at stake if I stay where I am?*
- *Who else am I impacting if this change is made or not made?*

What's Holding Me Back?

- *Are there habits, beliefs, or fears that might be getting in my way?*
- *What limiting stories do I need to let go of to move forward?*

My Goals for this area for the next 12 months

◎
◎
◎
◎
◎

TAKE INVENTORY: AWARENESS AND REFLECTION
CAREER

Take a moment to reflect deeply and honestly as you answer the following questions. These will help you gain clarity on where you are right now and create a clear vision for where you want to go.

On a scale of 1-10 (10 being completely satisfied), where would you rate your satisfaction with this area of life RIGHT NOW?

1 2 3 4 5 6 7 8 9 10

- *What does this area of my life currently look and feel like?*
- *What's working well?*
- *What's not working or feels out of alignment?*

_____

_____

_____

_____

_____

Where Do I Want to Be in One Year?
- *What specific improvements or changes do I want to see in this area?*
- *How do I want to feel in this area of my life one year from now?*
- *What would success in this area look like to me?*

_____

_____

_____

_____

_____

If I were to achieve this vision, what would I rate this area of my life then on the same 1-10 scale?

1 2 3 4 5 6 7 8 9 10

_____

_____

_____

TAKE INVENTORY: AWARENESS AND REFLECTION
CAREER

Why Does This Matter to Me?

- *Why is this goal or change important to me?*
- *How would achieving this improve my life overall?*
- *What's at stake if I stay where I am?*
- *Who else am I impacting if this change is made or not made?*

What's Holding Me Back?

- *Are there habits, beliefs, or fears that might be getting in my way?*
- *What limiting stories do I need to let go of to move forward?*

My Goals for this area for the next 12 months

- ◎
- ◎
- ◎
- ◎
- ◎

TAKE INVENTORY: AWARENESS AND REFLECTION

FINANCES

Take a moment to reflect deeply and honestly as you answer the following questions. These will help you gain clarity on where you are right now and create a clear vision for where you want to go.

On a scale of 1-10 (10 being completely satisfied), where would you rate your satisfaction with this area of life RIGHT NOW?

① ② ③ ④ ⑤ ⑥ ⑦ ⑧ ⑨ ⑩

- *What does this area of my life currently look and feel like?*
- *What's working well?*
- *What's not working or feels out of alignment?*

_____

_____

_____

_____

_____

Where Do I Want to Be in One Year?
- *What specific improvements or changes do I want to see in this area?*
- *How do I want to feel in this area of my life one year from now?*
- *What would success in this area look like to me?*

_____

_____

_____

_____

_____

If I were to achieve this vision, what would I rate this area of my life then on the same 1-10 scale?

① ② ③ ④ ⑤ ⑥ ⑦ ⑧ ⑨ ⑩

_____

_____

_____

TAKE INVENTORY: AWARENESS AND REFLECTION
FINANCES

Why Does This Matter to Me?
- *Why is this goal or change important to me?*
- *How would achieving this improve my life overall?*
- *What's at stake if I stay where I am?*
- *Who else am I impacting if this change is made or not made?*

What's Holding Me Back?
- *Are there habits, beliefs, or fears that might be getting in my way?*
- *What limiting stories do I need to let go of to move forward?*

My Goals for this area for the next 12 months

TAKE INVENTORY: AWARENESS AND REFLECTION
SPIRITUALITY / PURPOSE

Take a moment to reflect deeply and honestly as you answer the following questions. These will help you gain clarity on where you are right now and create a clear vision for where you want to go.

On a scale of 1-10 (10 being completely satisfied), where would you rate your satisfaction with this area of life RIGHT NOW?

1 2 3 4 5 6 7 8 9 10

- *What does this area of my life currently look and feel like?*
- *What's working well?*
- *What's not working or feels out of alignment?*

_____

_____

_____

_____

_____

Where Do I Want to Be in One Year?
- *What specific improvements or changes do I want to see in this area?*
- *How do I want to feel in this area of my life one year from now?*
- *What would success in this area look like to me?*

_____

_____

_____

_____

_____

If I were to achieve this vision, what would I rate this area of my life then on the same 1-10 scale?

1 2 3 4 5 6 7 8 9 10

_____

_____

_____

TAKE INVENTORY: AWARENESS AND REFLECTION
SPIRITUALITY / PURPOSE

Why Does This Matter to Me?
- *Why is this goal or change important to me?*
- *How would achieving this improve my life overall?*
- *What's at stake if I stay where I am?*
- *Who else am I impacting if this change is made or not made?*

What's Holding Me Back?
- *Are there habits, beliefs, or fears that might be getting in my way?*
- *What limiting stories do I need to let go of to move forward?*

My Goals for this area for the next 12 months

◎
◎
◎
◎
◎

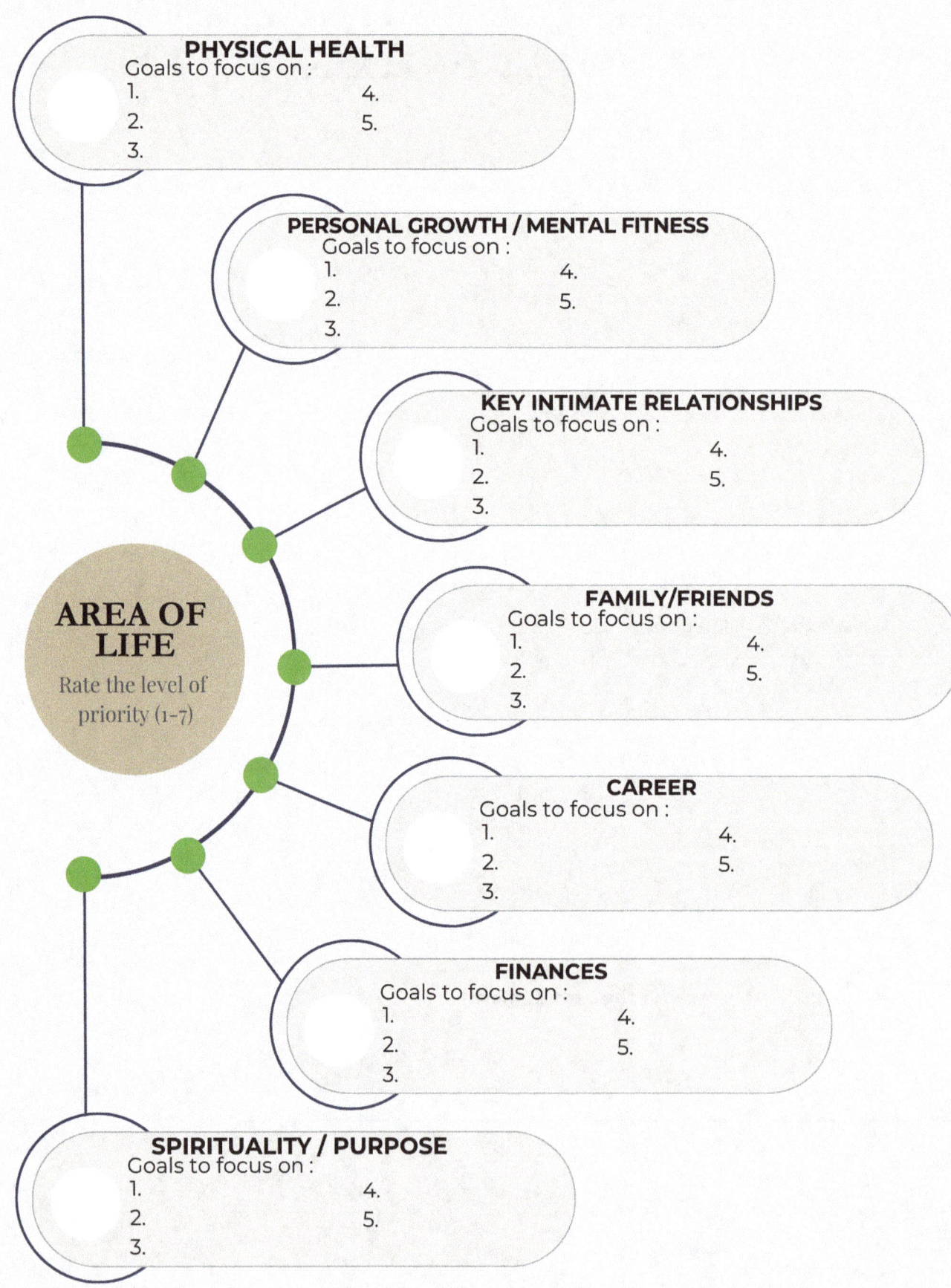

PHYSICAL HEALTH
Goals to focus on :
1.   4.
2.   5.
3.

PERSONAL GROWTH / MENTAL FITNESS
Goals to focus on :
1.   4.
2.   5.
3.

KEY INTIMATE RELATIONSHIPS
Goals to focus on :
1.   4.
2.   5.
3.

FAMILY/FRIENDS
Goals to focus on :
1.   4.
2.   5.
3.

AREA OF LIFE
Rate the level of priority (1-7)

CAREER
Goals to focus on :
1.   4.
2.   5.
3.

FINANCES
Goals to focus on :
1.   4.
2.   5.
3.

SPIRITUALITY / PURPOSE
Goals to focus on :
1.   4.
2.   5.
3.

PAUSE.
REFLECT.
RESET.

HOW DID I GET HERE?

These self-reflective questions can open up valuable insights into the choices and experiences that have brought you to where you are today. When we take the time to understand our journey and what truly drives us, we empower ourselves to make intentional choices moving forward—building a life that's deeply aligned with our values and aspirations.

Don't feel you need to answer all of these questions. Review them and see which ones resonate with you? Which ones make you a little uncomfortable and whisper to you "avoid it". I encourage you to kindly and gently lean in and sit with yourself on those questions - the part of you that wants to keep things as they are, not as you wish them to be, may start giving you thoughts to sabotage your progress.   Imagine that you are in the space of a trusted and loving friend (i'm happy to hold that space for you) and you are an explorer excited for their expedition.

You may choose to come back and answer more questions as a later time - whatever you choose, it's the right decision.

What were my earliest aspirations and goals?
What did I want to BE, DO, or HAVE?

_____

_____

_____

What key decisions or turning points led me to where I am today?
Were these decisions aligned with my values and long-term vision?

_____

_____

_____

Have external influences or societal expectations played a significant role in
shaping my path? How much agency did I have in making these decisions?

_____

_____

_____

Did I encounter any unexpected opportunities or challenges that altered my
course? How did I respond to these situations, and what did I learn from them?

_____

_____

_____

Have I been proactive in pursuing my goals and dreams, or have I allowed myself to be held back? If I have, what specifically has held me back? What specific beliefs or fears may have gotten in the way?

_____

_____

_____

How have my experiences and interactions with others impacted my journey? Have these relationships been supportive or detrimental to my growth?

_____

_____

_____

How do my current relationships impact my pursuit of my goals?

_____

_____

_____

Have I taken time for self-reflection along the way, or have I been on autopilot, simply going through the motions without conscious consideration of my path?

_____

_____

_____

Do I feel a sense of fulfillment and purpose in my current situation, or do I sense that there is a misalignment between where I am and where I want to be?

_____

_____

_____

What achievements and milestones have I reached?
Have I taken the time to celebrate them, or am I overly focused on the
destination rather than the journey?

_____

_____

_____

How have I dealt with setbacks and failures in my life? Have these experiences
motivated me to persevere or caused me to doubt my abilities?

_____

_____

_____

Are there any dreams or aspirations that I have put on hold or abandoned
altogether? What factors led to this decision, and is there a possibility of
revisiting these dreams?

_____

_____

_____

Have I taken risks and stepped outside of my comfort zone to pursue growth and
new experiences?

_____

_____

_____

Have I recognized and acknowledged my strengths and unique qualities? How have these attributes contributed to my current situation? What strengths and unique qualities am I not honoring?

_____

_____

_____

How has my perspective and outlook on life evolved over time? Have there been any significant shifts in my values or priorities that have influenced my path?

_____

_____

_____

What aspects of my current situation bring me joy and fulfillment, and what areas do I feel need improvement or adjustment?

_____

_____

_____

Have I sought guidance or support from mentors, coaches, or advisors along the way? How has this external guidance impacted my decisions and growth?

_____

_____

_____

Harness My Vision :
Dreaming Big and Setting Goals

Now that you've taken a good, honest look at where you are, it's time to focus on what's next—*where you want to go*. This is where we dream big, get bold, and dig into what lights you up. Your vision isn't just some fluffy idea; it's your anchor when life feels chaotic and your compass when you're figuring out your next move.

But here's the deal: this vision has to come from *you*. Not what others expect, not what feels "safe," and definitely not what someone else thinks you "should" want. This is about tapping into what *you* desire—the kind of life that gets you excited to wake up in the morning.

In this chapter, you'll find powerful exercises designed to help you uncover what you really want. These aren't surface-level goals or vague ideas; this is about connecting to your deepest desires. Give yourself permission to dream without limits. Even if it feels big or scary, write it down. Once your vision is clear, you'll have the foundation to start designing the roadmap to get there.

Lean into this process—your vision is the spark that will ignite everything to come. Let's go find it.

"Create the highest, grandest vision possible for your life, because you become what you believe."
— *Oprah Winfrey*

Lessons from the Shelf

Listen to MB share the story of the two shelves by scanning the QR code.

Imagine you're at a stage in life where you're down to the essentials—just the things that can fit on **two shelves.** These aren't just objects; they're the heartbeat of your story, each piece capturing the people, experiences, and passions that have defined your life.

The challenge: with only two shelves, what will you choose?

Each item should have deep significance—a reminder of moments and relationships that shaped you. Maybe it's a photo of loved ones who've been your anchors or mentors who profoundly impacted you. Perhaps it's a symbol of a life milestone, like a book you authored, a photo of that bucket-list safari, or a memento from a special family vacation. You may choose something that represents a cause, a passion, or a hobby that has defined your purpose and joy. The items you see may be things you WANT to accomplish or experience in the future.

With just two feet of space, you're capturing the essence of what truly mattered to you. When you look at these shelves, the sight is powerful—a storyboard of your life, distilled into a few meaningful objects that move you deeply.

REFLECTIONS

1. What are the items I would like to see on my two shelves? Describe it in as much detail as you can.

2. What do these items represent about the most important people, experiences, and values in my life?

3. Which memories or moments are essential to include in this display of my life story? What matters most?

The Second Set of Shelves

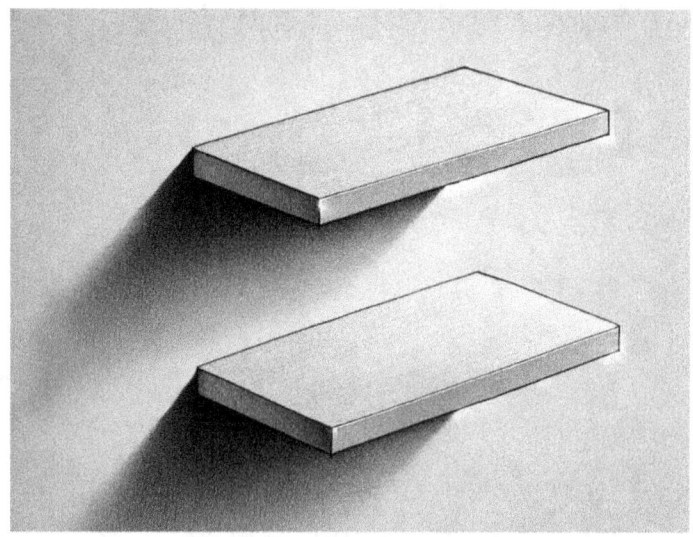

Now that you've identified who and what matters most in your life, it's time to flip the perspective. Imagine a second set of shelves—this time, they aren't yours. Instead, these are the shelves of others, and the question is:

Whose shelves do you want to be on? And for what purpose?

Consider: who you want to impact so deeply that you've earned a place in their lives, their memories, and their stories. This isn't about physical objects; it's about the legacy you leave behind. Think about the ripple effect of your life—do you want to be on the "shelves" of students you've taught, individuals touched by your philanthropy, or people whose lives changed because of the jobs you created? Perhaps it's family, friends, or loved ones who look at a photo of you and feel something lasting and true because of the role you played in their lives.

As you reflect, remember: this is a metaphor for the impact you hope to make. Think deeply about the values, actions, and relationships that will carry your story forward. What will they feel, remember, and know because of you?

REFLECTIONS

1. Whose shelves do I want to be on, and what do I want to represent in their lives?

2. What impact do I hope to have on the people I care about most?

REFLECTIONS

3. How do I want to be remembered by my family, friends, or community?

4. What legacy am I leaving through my work, actions, and relationships?

Discovering Your Purpose and Legacy

By : MB Gustitus

Are You Living the Life That Leads to Your Shelves?

As you picture these shelves and the experiences, relationships, and impact they represent, ask yourself: Does my current life reflect this vision? Am I taking steps today to create the story I want these shelves to tell? Where are the gaps?

Consider: **Are the choices I'm making today filling those shelves with meaning, purpose, and the legacy I truly want?**

CREATIVE PAUSE

This space is yours! Sketch, doodle, or jot down whatever comes to mind
—no rules, just creativity!

REFLECTIONS

1. Are there meaningful experiences or relationships I haven't yet prioritized but want to?

2. How do these shelves make me feel about the life I've lived so far?

3. Am I living and acting in a way today that will earn me a place on these shelves? What can I do to align more closely with this vision?

Design Your Best Life

Your *THRIVE Blueprint* is more than just a plan—it's a powerful way to bridge the gap between where you are and where you want to be. Neuroscience tells us that when we vividly imagine our future and align our actions with that vision, we activate the brain's reticular activating system (RAS). The RAS acts like a spotlight, filtering information and bringing attention to what you focus on. For example, have you ever learned a new word and suddenly heard it everywhere? That's your RAS in action, tuning your brain to notice what's relevant to your current focus. By creating a clear vision of your future self, you're teaching your brain to filter out distractions and highlight opportunities that align with your goals. This book will help you get intentional about your life, align your daily actions with your values, and set meaningful goals that move you closer to the thriving life you're meant to live. Let's map out your best life—step by step, one inspired action at a time. You've got this!

"Create the highest, grandest vision possible for your life, because you become what you believe." —Oprah Winfrey

The following pages will guide you step-by-step to create your THRIVE Blueprint, helping you envision your future, align your actions, and set clear goals to live your best life by design.

"The best way to predict your future is to create it." —Abraham Lincoln

(1) Envision Your Future Self (BE)

Your *Future Self* is the best version of you—the person you aspire to become. This step is about creating a clear and inspiring vision of the thriving life you want to design. When you vividly imagine your future, you activate your brain's Reticular Activating System (RAS), helping you focus on opportunities and actions that align with your goals. The more detailed and intentional your vision, the more empowered you'll feel to start making it a reality.

Part 1: Describe Your Future Self

Your Future Self encompasses four key areas of life: Spiritual, Mental, Emotional, and Physical. Take time to reflect and write about who you want to be in each area.

Prompts to Guide You:

1. **Spiritual:**

   How do you want to show up in the world? What grounds you and gives you purpose?

   Example :
   - *I am grounded in my purpose and show up with energy and gratitude.*
   - *I practice mindfulness daily and focus on meaningful relationships.*

2. **Mental:**

   What does your thought life look like? What do you focus on and believe about yourself?

   Example :
   - *I prioritize learning and reflection.*
   - *My thoughts are clear and focused on growth and possibility.*

3. **Emotional:**

   How do you want to feel each day? How do you nurture your emotional well-being?

   Example :
   - *I feel joy, love, and peace.*
   - *I journal regularly and practice self-compassion.*

4. **Physical:**

   What does your health look like? How do you care for your body?
   Example :
   - *I am strong and energetic.*
   - *I exercise regularly, eat nutritious meals, and get enough rest.*

Your Turn

Use the space below to write your own descriptions of your Future Self.

Spiritual:

_____
_____
_____
_____
_____
_____

Mental :

_____
_____
_____
_____
_____
_____

Emotional:

_____
_____
_____
_____
_____

Physical:

_____
_____
_____
_____
_____

Part 2: Aligning with Your Future Self – Start, Stop, Continue

Now that you've envisioned your Future Self, it's time to identify the habits and behaviors that will help you align with this vision. This is where you get practical —reflecting on what to start, what to stop, and what to continue doing to move closer to your best life.

Why This Matters:

Every habit or behavior you choose to keep, change, or let go of either supports or detracts from your future self. By doing this exercise, you'll clarify the shifts you need to make to build momentum and stay aligned with your vision.

Instructions:

1. **START :**
   Based on your Future Self, what new habits, actions, or behaviors should you begin doing to align with your vision?

   Example Response :
   - *Begin waking up 30 minutes earlier to meditate and set my intentions for the day.*
   - *Plan weekly meals to eat healthier and stay consistent.*
   - *Schedule time each week for personal growth, like reading or taking a course.*

2. **STOP :**
   What habits, actions, or behaviors are holding you back and need to be left behind?

   Example Response :
   - *Stop scrolling through social media late at night and losing sleep.*
   - *Stop saying "yes" to commitments that don't align with my priorities.*
   - *Stop eating takeout multiple times a week and skipping workouts.*

3. **CONTINUE:**
   What habits, actions, or behaviors are already aligned with your Future Self and should be maintained or enhanced?

   Example Response :
   - *Continue exercising three times a week and prioritizing my health.*
   - *Continue journaling each night to process emotions and reflect on my day.*
   - *Continue practicing gratitude daily to maintain a positive mindset.*

Your Turn

Use the space below to reflect on what to START, STOP, and CONTINUE doing based on your Future Self.

START :

_____

_____

_____

_____

_____

_____

STOP :

_____

_____

_____

_____

_____

_____

_____

CONTINUE:

_____

_____

_____

_____

_____

_____

Reflect & Release :
Clearing Limiting Beliefs

Once you become aware of what's holding you back, you gain the power to break free from it."

—Jay Shetty

Overcoming Limiting Beliefs: Facing Your Mindset Monsters

This section is about confronting the **Mindset Monsters** that have been holding you back. You know the ones—they show up as whispers of doubt, right when you start dreaming big or imagining something extraordinary for your life. They might say things like, *"You're not good enough,"* *"Who are you to want this?"* or *"What if you fail?"* These aren't facts. They're stories your mind has created over time—stories that no longer serve you. The good news? You have the power to face these monsters, challenge their grip on you, and rewrite the narrative into something empowering and true.

STEP 1 ▶ Name Your Mindset Monster

When you dared to dream big during your reflection and vision exercises, did a negative thought or voice show up to challenge you? That's your Mindset Monster rearing its head. These monsters thrive in the shadows of your subconscious, where they feed on fear and self-doubt. It's time to call them out and take away their power.

Examples of Mindset Monsters:

- When envisioning a healthier, stronger you, your monster might say, *"You've tried before and failed—why would this time be any different?"*
- While dreaming of an exciting career change, it might whisper, *"You're not smart enough for that kind of success."*
- Thinking about financial freedom could trigger, *"People like you don't get to have that kind of life."*

Exercise:

- Write down one limiting belief or thought that popped up during your reflection or vision work.
- Name your monster. For example: *The Perfectionist, The Critic, or The Doubter.* Giving it a name helps you separate it from yourself.
- Describe what it's saying to you. What fears is this monster trying to reinforce?

STEP 2 ▶ Uncover What Feeds Your Monster

Mindset Monsters aren't random—they're fueled by old beliefs and stories you've been carrying, often since childhood or significant emotional experiences.

Exercise:

- Reflect on the limiting thought you identified. What belief is fueling this monster? For example:

  If your monster says, *"You're not smart enough,"* the belief might be, *"I have to be perfect to succeed."*
  If it says, *"You'll fail,"* the belief might be, *"Taking risks leads to pain."*

- Write down these beliefs, even if they feel uncomfortable or illogical. Awareness is the first step to change.

STEP 3 ▶ Face the Consequences of Your Monster

Mindset Monsters don't just hang out in your mind—they impact your life in profound ways. Understanding their consequences helps you see why it's time to let them go.

Exercise:

- Reflect on how this monster has influenced your thoughts, actions, and decisions. How has it affected your relationships, confidence, career, or health?
- Imagine your life 1, 5, and 10 years from now if this monster remains in control. How much more space will it take up? What will it cost you emotionally, physically, and mentally?
- Lean into this exercise. Let yourself feel the weight of these consequences—because if it doesn't move you, *it won't move you.*

STEP 4 ▸ Challenge Your Monster

Now it's time to take the fight to your monster. This is where you break down its arguments and prove that its story doesn't hold up.

Exercise:

- Write down evidence that disproves your monster's claims. For example:

  "I'm not good enough" can be countered with times you achieved something despite fear or doubt.

  "I'll fail if I try" might be challenged by moments where you tried, learned, and grew—even if it didn't go perfectly.

- Think of someone you admire who faced similar doubts and succeeded. What lessons can you take from their journey?
- Write out your findings. Every piece of evidence weakens the monster's hold on you.

STEP 5 ▸ Rewrite the Script and Tame Your Monster

Your monster has had its say—now it's your turn. By replacing its outdated script with a new, empowering belief, you take back control of your mindset.

Exercise:
- Write a new belief to replace the limiting one. For example:

  Monster's belief: *"You're not good enough."*

  Your belief: *"I am capable and learning every day."*

- Identify one action you can take today that supports this belief and begins taming the monster.
- Create an affirmation to reinforce your new belief daily. For example: *"I am worthy of success, and I take bold steps toward my goals."*

Conquer Your Mindset Monster   **Date :** _____

1 Write down one limiting thought that came up in your reflection or vision. Describe what it is saying to you. What fear is this monster trying to create or reinforce? Now...GIVE IT A NAME!

2 Now go deeper. What <u>belief</u> is fueling this monster? Write down these beliefs, even if they feel uncomfortable or illogical.

3 Reflect on how this monster has influenced your thoughts, actions, and decisions. How has it affected your relationships, confidence, career, or health? What has it encouraged you to do? or NOT do?

- Imagine your life 1, 5, and 10 years from now if this monster remains in control. How much more space will it take up? What will it cost you emotionally, physically, and mentally?

Conquer Your Mindset Monster

Date : _____

 Write down evidence that what this Mindset Monster is telling you is actually *TRUE* (chances are you can't find it), or evidence that disproves this Story entirely! -
Write out your findings.

 - Write a new belief to replace the limiting one.
- Identify one action you can take today that supports this belief and begins taming the monster.
- Create an affirmation to reinforce your new belief daily.

Intentional Action :
Daily Habits
and Actions

"A goal without a plan is just a wish."

—Antoine de Saint-Exupéry

The THRIVE Blueprint

Creating a healthier, stronger version of yourself starts with a clear plan. The *THRIVE Blueprint* will guide you to identify your goals, focus on key priorities, and create actionable strategies to achieve them. This roadmap will help you build consistency, stay motivated, and turn your vision into reality.

"You have to decide what your highest priorities are and have the courage—pleasantly, smilingly, unapologetically—to say no to other things. And the way you do that is by having a bigger yes burning inside."

—Stephen Covey

How to Complete Your THRIVE Blueprint

1 . Set Your Goal

Write down your specific goal.

Make it measurable, realistic, and inspiring.

2 . Define 3 Key Priorities

Break your goal into three main focus areas.

These priorities should address the essential components required to achieve it.

3 . Create 5 Actionable Strategies for Each Priority

For each priority, write down five specific, actionable steps you'll take to move closer to your goal.

4 . Track Your Progress

Keep your THRIVE Blueprint visible—use the THRIVE in 90 journal to keep your momentum going for a powerful 90 days!

Commit time weekly to celebrate progress, reflect on challenges, and adjust strategies as needed.

Thrive Blueprint Example

ONE GOAL
I want to lose 20 pounds and increase my energy within the next 6 months.

Priority #1 **NUTRITION**	Priority #2 **FITNESS**	Priority #3 **MINDSET AND HABITS**
Strategies :	Strategies :	Strategies :
1. Meal prep each week to include balanced, whole-food meals. 2. Drink at least 64 ounces of water daily. 3. Reduce processed foods and focus on lean proteins, healthy fats, and vegetables. 4. Keep a food journal to track eating habits and stay mindful. 5. Replace sugary drinks with unsweetened alternatives like herbal tea.	1. Walk 10,000 steps a day, five days a week. 2. Strength train three times a week to build muscle and boost metabolism. 3. Try one new physical activity, like a yoga class or hiking, to keep fitness fun. 4. Set a reminder to stretch for 10 minutes every morning. 5. Track workouts to monitor progress and celebrate milestones.	1. Meditate for 5–10 minutes each morning to reduce stress and set a positive tone. 2. Create a daily affirmation: "I am healthy, strong, and making progress every day." 3. Reflect on your wins each evening to stay motivated. 4. Partner with an accountability buddy to stay consistent. 5. Set up small, non-food rewards for milestones (like new workout gear or a massage).

My Thrive Blueprint

MY ONE GOAL

why this goal matters to me...

Priority #1	Priority #2	Priority #3
5 Strategies :	5 Strategies :	5 Strategies :

Define Your Small Daily Actions (SDA'S)

Small Daily actions (SDA's) are the habits and routines that align with your Future Self. These are the small, consistent steps that build a thriving life. They are actions you DO because that is who you ARE, they do not have an "end".

Instructions:

1. Reflect on the habits and actions your Future Self would prioritize.
2. Write down 3–5 daily actions you will commit to consistently.

Example Actions:

- Meditate for 10 minutes every morning.
- Exercise for 30 minutes, five days a week.
- Write down three things I'm grateful for each evening.
- Read or learn for 30 minutes daily.
- Drink 64 ounces of water every day.

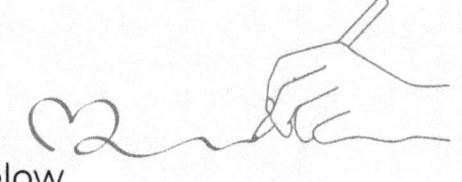

Your Turn

Write down your small daily actions below.

Spiritual:

1. ....
2. ....
3. ....
4. ....
5. ....

Mental :

1. ....
2. ....
3. ....
4. ....
5. ....

Emotional:

1. ....
2. ....
3. ....
4. ....
5. ....

Physical:

1. ....
2. ....
3. ....
4. ....
5. ....

Why the THRIVE Blueprint Works

The *THRIVE Blueprint* simplifies your transformation by breaking it into clear, actionable steps. Focusing on three key areas helps you avoid overwhelm and ensures you're building a sustainable, balanced approach to achieve your goals. Consistency and intention are your secret weapons.

"Success is the sum of small efforts, repeated day in and day out."

—Robert Collier

THRIVE ACTION PLANNER

Managing Your Time and Attention: The THRIVE Way

Time and attention are your most valuable resources, and how you manage them will determine the success of your THRIVE Blueprint. This section will help you take control of your schedule, focus on what matters most, and avoid distractions that derail your progress. Using tools like time blocking and prioritization, you'll create a system that aligns your daily actions with your goals.

Why This Matters

Research shows that people who set clear priorities and protect their time are more productive and less stressed. The key is to manage yourself—not just your time—by focusing on the activities that align with your goals and values. This section is about learning to say yes to what matters and no to what doesn't, so you can focus on the 20% of activities that will create 80% of your results (Pareto Principle).

"The key is in not spending time, but in investing it." —*Stephen R. Covey*

⟳ STEP 1: IDENTIFY YOUR BIG ROCKS

Your *Big Rocks* are the priorities that align with your Future Self and make the biggest impact on your goals. These should focus on your most meaningful tasks, not just the urgent ones.

Exercise:

1. Write down your top 3–5 Big Rocks for the year. These should reflect your major goals.
   - Example:
     - Build a healthier body (physical health).
     - Strengthen relationships with family (emotional connection).
     - Launch a new business (career).

2. Break these Big Rocks into monthly and weekly priorities.
   - Example:
     - Monthly: Attend four family dinners.
     - Weekly: Plan one quality family activity.

THRIVE ACTION PLAN

ANNUAL BIG ROCKS

- ○
- ○
- ○
- ○
- ○

MONTHLY PRIORITIES

	✓	✗	➡
	Completed	did not complete	move to next month

- ○
- ○
- ○
- ○
- ○

WEEKLY ACTIONS

WEEK 1 ✓✗➡	WEEK 2 ✓✗➡	WEEK 3 ✓✗➡	WEEK 4 ✓✗➡

⟳ STEP 2: TIME BLOCKING

Time blocking is the practice of scheduling specific times for your most important tasks. This keeps your day purposeful and aligned with your priorities.

Instructions:

1. Identify your top 2–3 daily priorities (your "have-to-do" list).
2. Block uninterrupted time on your calendar to work on these priorities.
3. Be purposeful about when you schedule tasks based on your energy levels (e.g., high-focus tasks in the morning).
4. Protect your time by treating these blocks as non-negotiable appointments.

Example Schedule:

- 8:00–9:00 AM: Exercise (physical health).
- 9:30–11:30 AM: Work on business project (career).
- 6:00–7:00 PM: Family dinner (relationships).

DAILY TIME-BLOCKING

"It's not about having time; it's about making time." —Unknown

12:00 AM

1:00 AM

2:00 AM

3:00 AM

4:00 AM

5:00 AM

6:00 AM

7:00 AM

8:00 AM

9:00 AM

10:00 AM

11:00 AM

12:00 PM

1:00 PM

2:00 PM

3:00 PM

4:00 PM

5:00 PM

6:00 PM

7:00 PM

8:00 PM

9:00 PM

10:00 PM

11:00 PM

STEP 3: DELEGATE AND SIMPLIFY

You can't do everything, and you shouldn't try. Delegating or leveraging tools and systems allows you to focus on what truly matters.

Exercise:

1. List 3–5 tasks or responsibilities you could delegate to others or automate with tools.

    ○ Example:

        ▪ Hire a housecleaner for bi-weekly cleaning.

        ▪ Use a meal delivery service to save time on cooking.

        ▪ Delegate administrative tasks to an assistant.

2. Reflect on how delegating these tasks will free up your time and energy for your Big Rocks.

"You can do anything, but not everything."
—David Allen

DELEGATING OR LEVERAGING

TASKS TO DELEGATE	WHO OR WHAT SYSTEM WILL HANDLE

 # STEP 4: REFLECT AND ADJUST

Managing your time and attention isn't a one-and-done process.
Regular reflection will help you stay aligned and adapt to changes.

Instructions:

1. At the end of each week, review your schedule and Action Plan and ask:
   - What worked well this week?
   - What changes do I need to make next week?
   - How much time did I spend on Quadrant 2 activities?
   - Did I focus on my Big Rocks?
   - Where did I let distractions steal my time?

2. Make adjustments to your time-blocking and priorities as needed.

WEEKLY REVIEW

DATE _____

THINGS THAT WORKED WELL
THIS WEEK
_____

HOW MUCH TIME DID I SPEND ON
QUADRANT 2 ACTIVITIES?
_____

CHANGES I NEED TO MAKE NEXT WEEK
_____

_____

_____

_____

_____

WHERE DID I LET DISTRACTIONS
STEAL MY TIME?
_____

DID I FOCUS ON MY BIG ROCKS?

☆ ☆ ☆ ☆ ☆

The THRIVE Time Management Matrix Exercise

This exercise will help you focus your time and energy on what truly matters by categorizing your tasks into four quadrants: **Necessity**, **Productivity**, **Distraction**, and **Waste**. Based on Stephen Covey's time management matrix, this tool empowers you to prioritize effectively and eliminate unnecessary activities that drain your focus.

❖

Why This Matters

Time is your most limited resource, and how you spend it determines your success. This exercise will help you identify high-priority activities (Quadrants 1 and 2), avoid distractions (Quadrant 3), and eliminate time-wasters (Quadrant 4), ensuring that you align your daily actions with your *THRIVE Blueprint*.

"Most of us spend too much time on what is urgent and not enough time on what is important."
—Stephen R. Covey

Instructions for the THRIVE Time Management Exercise

1. Brainstorm Your Current Activities

1. Write down all the tasks, activities, and commitments you currently spend time on.
2. Include everything—work, personal life, routines, and even seemingly small distractions like scrolling social media.

2. Categorize Your Tasks into Quadrants

Use the following definitions to place each activity into one of the four quadrants:

- **Quadrant 1: Necessity (Manage)**

  These are urgent and important tasks that require immediate attention.

  - Examples: Deadlines, emergencies, solving crises.

- **Quadrant 2: Productivity (Focus)**

  These are important but not urgent tasks that support long-term growth.

  - Examples: Planning, skill development, building relationships.

- **Quadrant 3: Distraction (Avoid)**

  These are urgent but not important tasks that distract from your priorities.

  - Examples: Interruptions, unnecessary meetings, emails.

- **Quadrant 4: Waste (Eliminate)**

  These are neither urgent nor important and should be minimized or eliminated.

  - Examples: Mindless TV, excessive social media, busywork.

TIME MANAGEMENT
MATRIX TEMPLATE

NECESSITY
Quadrant 1

PRODUCTIVITY
Quadrant 2

DISTRACTION
Quadrant 3

WASTE
Quadrant 4

3. Reflect and Adjust

1. Once you've categorized your tasks, reflect on where most of your time is spent.

2. Answer these questions:

> **Where am I spending most of my time?**

> **How can I invest more time in Quadrant 2 activities?**

> **What steps can I take to reduce Quadrant 3 and 4 distractions?**

4. Create an Action Plan

1. **Focus on Quadrant 2:**
   - Identify three specific actions you can take this week to invest more time in important, non-urgent activities.
   - Example: Schedule 30 minutes daily for planning, personal development, or exercise.

2. **Reduce Quadrant 3 and 4 Activities:**
   - Identify distractions and time-wasters to eliminate or delegate.
   - Example: Turn off unnecessary notifications or set limits for social media use.

3. **Plan for Quadrant 1:**
   - Write down strategies to manage urgent tasks more effectively.
   - Example: Break larger tasks into smaller, manageable steps to avoid last-minute emergencies.

THOUGHTS TO THRIVE

Your time and attention are your greatest resources, and how you use them will determine your success. By focusing on your Big Rocks—the priorities that matter most—you're creating space for what truly drives progress. Remember, the goal isn't to fill your days with endless tasks; it's to align your actions with your vision and create meaningful impact.

As you move forward, use tools like the THRIVE Action Planner and Time Management Matrix to manage your time with intention. Simplify where you can, protect what matters, and stay focused on what moves you closer to your goals.

"Time is what we want most, but what we use worst."
—William Penn

Value Alignment :
Living Authentically

"When your values are clear, your decisions become easier." —Roy E. Disney

At the heart of every decision you make, every goal you set, and every path you choose are your **core values**. These values are the foundation of who you are—they shape your behavior, guide your actions, and give meaning to your life. When you align with your values, you feel fulfilled and authentic. When you stray from them, life can feel unbalanced, uncertain, or even empty. This section is about getting crystal clear on what truly matters to you so you can live with purpose, direction, and confidence.

Identifying your core values isn't always easy. Many of us have been so focused on the expectations of others or the demands of daily life that we haven't stopped to ask ourselves: *What's most important to me?* This is your opportunity to pause and dig deep, uncovering the guiding principles that reflect who you are at your core. Through a series of exercises, we'll explore what drives you, prioritize your values, and turn them into actionable commitments.

As you go through this process, remember: this is not about judgment or perfection—it's about understanding. Your values are already within you; we're simply shining a light on them.

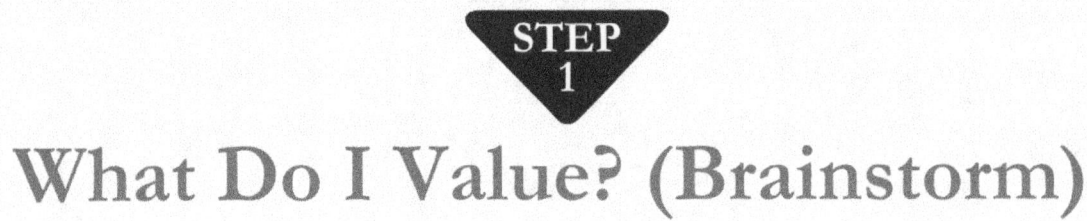

What Do I Value? (Brainstorm)

We begin by casting a wide net to identify the values that resonate with you.

Exercise :

1. Select an area of your life you want to focus on (Physical/Mental Health, Personal Growth, Key Intimate Relationships, Family/Friends, Career, Finances, Spirituality/Purpose) - write your area of focus here.

2. Ask yourself: *What's important to me in this area (use value based words)?* Repeat the question three times to uncover deeper layers.

Condense Your List

After brainstorming, you'll likely have a long list of values. It's time to simplify and focus on what matters most.

1. Group similar values together. You may have many words on your list that represent the same thing to you...select the one that resonates the most and eliminate the others. You should be left with a list where every words represents something unique, and has its own "picture" in your mind.

2. Narrow your list down to 5–7 values that feel most meaningful to you.

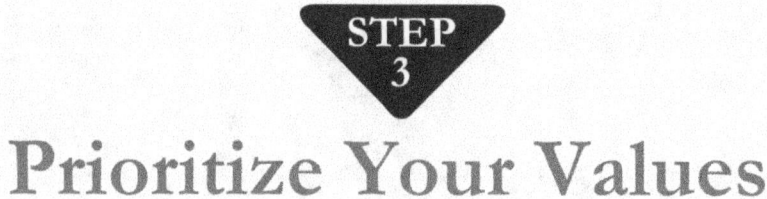

Prioritize Your Values

Now that you've identified your core values, it's time to rank them.
This helps you understand which values guide your decisions most powerfully.

1. Order your 5–7 values from most important to least important. Ask: *If I could only honor one of these, which would it be?* Use this process to refine your hierarchy.

2. Sit with your final list and ask yourself: *Does this feel right? Does this reflect who I am and who I want to be?*

Define Your Values

Your values aren't just words—they hold personal meaning unique to you.
Defining them brings clarity and depth.

Exercise :

1. For each of your top values, write what it means to you. How do you know when this value is being met? How do you know when it isn't?

STEP 5

Living Your Values with Intention

Now that you've uncovered and defined your core values, it's time to align your actions with them. This step is about honoring your values and creating boundaries that protect them.

Exercise :

START: Based on my vision and values, what am I currently not doing that I will commit to START

STOP: What I am currently doing that conflicts with my vision and values that I will commit to STOP

CONTINUE: What am I currently doing that *is* aligned with my vision and values that I intend to CONTINUE.

LOADING...

PROGRESS

—— over ——

PERFECTION

Evolve :
Celebrate Wins, Adapt, and Grow

Welcome to the final step of your THRIVE Blueprint: EVOLVE.

This is where we shift our focus from *doing* to *becoming*. You've done the work—gained clarity, set your vision, let go of limiting beliefs, built habits, and aligned your actions with your values. But here's the truth: transformation isn't a one-and-done deal. It's an ongoing process of growth, reflection, and adjustment.

This chapter is all about **celebrating how far you've come, learning from the journey, and continuously evolving into your highest self**. Because growth isn't about perfection—it's about progress, adaptability, and having the courage to keep moving forward, no matter what life throws your way.

STEP 1: CELEBRATE YOUR WINS – BIG & SMALL

Most people don't stop to acknowledge their progress. They're so focused on the *next thing* that they forget to appreciate how much they've already grown. Not here. Not in THRIVE.

Exercise: Your Celebration List

Instructions :

1. Flip back through your journal—your goals, actions, and reflections.

2. Write down 10 wins—big or small—that you've accomplished during this journey.

- Maybe you launched a new project, set better boundaries, or even just started believing in yourself again.

3. Under each win, write why it matters—how it made you feel, what it changed for you.

Example:

✓ Win: Spoke up in a meeting and shared my ideas.

✓ Why It Matters: I finally realized my voice is valuable, and I deserve to be heard.

WIN TRACKER

Win :
Why It Matters :

Win :
Why It Matters :

Win :
Why It Matters :

Win :
Why It Matters :

Win :
Why It Matters :

Win :
Why It Matters :

Win :
Why It Matters :

Win :
Why It Matters :

Win :
Why It Matters :

Win :
Why It Matters :

STEP 2:
EMBRACE THE LESSONS –
WHAT WORKED, WHAT DIDN'T?

Growth comes from experience—both the *wins and the challenges*. Every stumble, every pivot, every unexpected detour taught you something. It's time to extract those lessons.

Exercise: Lessons from the Journey

Instructions :

1. Reflect on moments when things didn't go as planned.

2. Ask yourself: What did I learn? How can I use this moving forward?

3. Write down at least three key lessons you've gained from this journey.

Example:

✓ **The Challenge:** I set too many goals at once and got overwhelmed.

✓ **The Lesson:** Focus on 1-2 major priorities at a time to build consistency.

✓ **The Shift:** I'll simplify my approach and celebrate small wins.

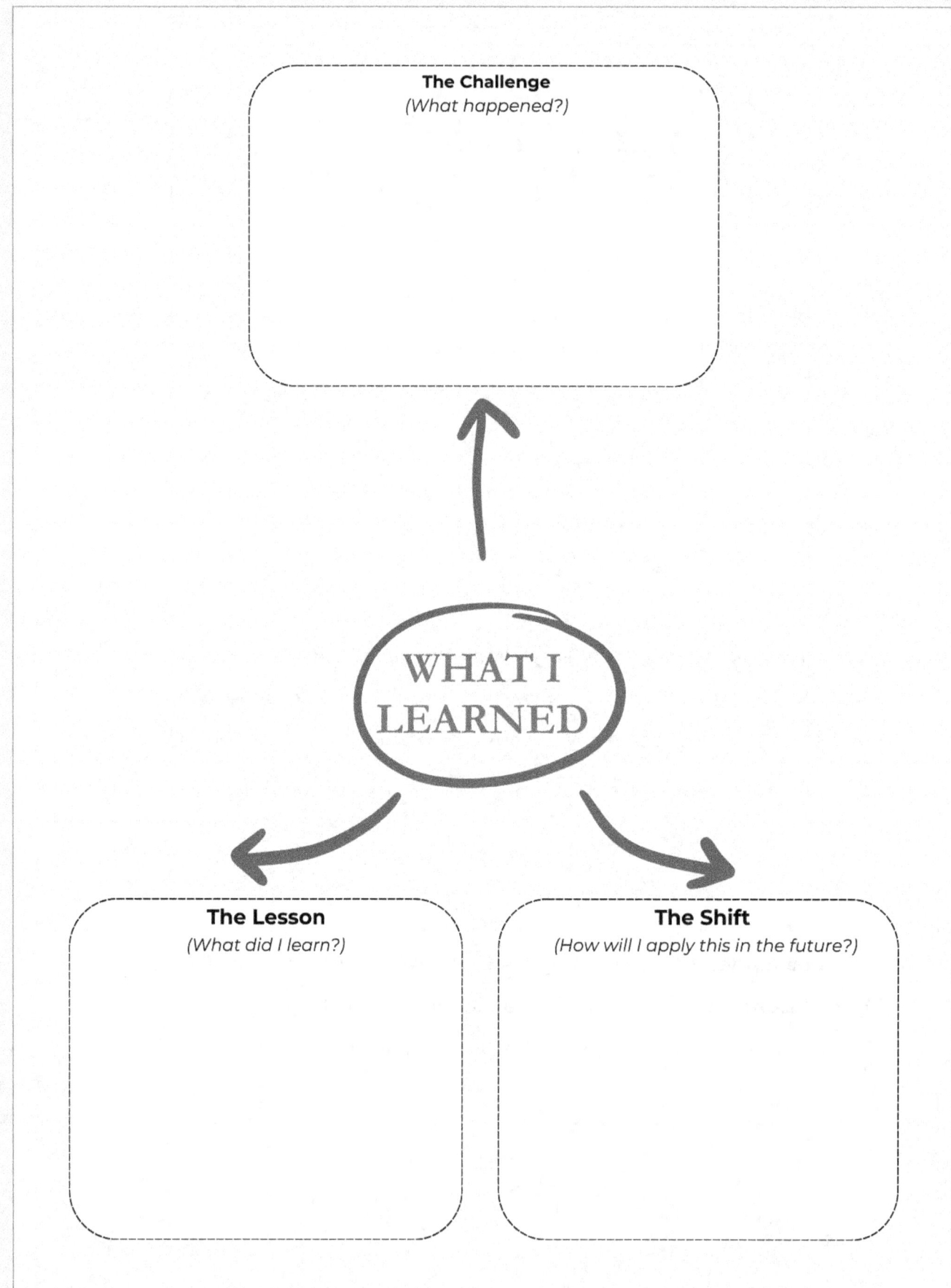

The Challenge
(What happened?)

WHAT I
LEARNED

The Lesson
(What did I learn?)

The Shift
(How will I apply this in the future?)

STEP 3:
ADAPT & RECOMMIT
TO YOUR GROWTH

Growth isn't linear. Life changes, priorities shift, and what worked for you six months ago might not be what you need now. That's not failure—that's evolution.

The Check-In & Reset

Instructions :

1. Take a moment to check in: **Are my goals and habits still aligned with who I want to become?**

2. If yes—amazing! If not, where do I need to adjust?

3. Rewrite or refine 1-3 goals that feel most relevant for the next season of your life.

What's still working?

What's no longer serving me?

What new goals feel aligned?

A LETTER FROM YOUR FUTURE SELF

Take a moment to imagine your Future Self—the person who has achieved the goals you're working toward. Write a letter from that version of you, offering encouragement, wisdom, and gratitude for the steps you're taking now to create the life you've envisioned.

KEEP THRIVING

Wow—look at you! You've made it to the end of this journey, and I couldn't be more proud of you. The fact that you showed up, did the work, and committed to creating real change speaks volumes about who you are and what you're capable of. You've taken intentional steps toward clarity, growth, and transformation—and that is something to celebrate. Thank you for trusting me and this process. It's been an honor to walk alongside you as you've built momentum toward your goals.

But let's be clear—this isn't the end. It's the beginning of a new chapter, one where you continue to grow, evolve, and thrive. You've built a foundation here, but the real magic comes from how you carry this forward into your everyday life. Keep leaning into the practices you've developed, revisit these pages when you need to refocus, and remember: you are capable of so much more than you've ever imagined.

I'm so excited for what's ahead for you. Keep dreaming, keep taking bold action, and most importantly, keep showing up for yourself. The best is yet to come, and I can't wait to see all that you create. You've got this, and I'm cheering you on every step of the way!

Much love,

About the Author

MaryBeth "MB" Gustitus is a no-nonsense, high-energy coach, facilitator, and founder of *Mile One Coaching*. With over three decades of experience in leadership, coaching, and personal development, MB has helped thousands of individuals and teams unlock their potential, get real with themselves, and create lasting transformation. Known for her ability to blend humor, straight talk, and actionable strategies, MB challenges people to stop making excuses and *own their sht**—because that's where real growth begins. As a Certified Integrative Coach, Master Practitioner of Neuro-Linguistic Programming (NLP), and Certified Behavioral Analyst specializing in DISC, she's passionate about empowering people to live with clarity, intention, and confidence. MB is on a mission to help people stop settling and *start thriving*.

This journal is her invitation to you: take ownership, lean in, and design the life you've always wanted.

MB Gustitus